NICK RANIERI

Perspectives: A Christmas Advent

Seeing Jesus Through Different Eyes

First edition

Editing by Sharon Ranieri, Hannah Hagen, and Kip Perry

Contents

Preface

It's been said that the great American preacher, Gardner C. Taylor, had an inscription placed behind the pulpit of his church for all preachers to see before opening the Word of God. The inscription was from John 12:21 and it read: "We would see Jesus." Dr. Taylor explained why he had that phrase inscribed:

> *The preacher needed to see that! Never mind your skill of oratory: "We would see Jesus." Do not dazzle us with your knowledge. We have come here to see Jesus. We are not hungry for your theories of life. "We would see Jesus." Never mind your positions and suppositions about what is or ought to be. "We would see Jesus."*[1]

Nothing is more important than seeing Jesus. In fact, that's the great hope of eternal life that "we will see him as he is" (1 John 3:2). We can learn facts and gain greater discipline and grow in kindness, but greater than all those things is that we see Jesus as he is. For as John points out in his letters, as we see Jesus we will be made like him. This Christmas season, may the Lord give you eyes to see him and ears to hear him. It's my prayer for you that through this study, the Holy Spirit would gift you greater clarity and deeper worship.

---

[1] Taylor, *The Words of Gardner Taylor: Sermons from the Middle Years, 1970–1980,* 2:130.

HOW TO USE THIS BOOK

Advent devotionals come in all shapes and sizes. This book is designed to be a tool for you to use individually or in community with others. There are five chapters in total, one for each Sunday of December and one to be used on either Christmas Eve or Christmas morning. If possible, I'd encourage you to read through each week in a family or community setting. Each chapter focuses on a different character within the Biblical narrative. It's often easy to simply look at Jesus through our eyes, but the goal of this advent is to help you see Jesus through the eyes of the people within the story. It's my hope that this will give you an expanded perspective of the Christmas story. Within each chapter you will find a few sections that are detailed below.

SCRIPTURE

It's important to start with Scripture. Not only is it where we find the Christmas story, but it's the very word of God. Therefore, it's more powerful and more important than anything I could possibly include in this book. As you enter this time, I urge you to prioritize this section and come to the words of God with excitement and expectation.

STORY

Each chapter contains an imaginative story to help you see and feel what the characters may have been experiencing. There's a lot of artistic license used in these stories and they are not intended to be taken as literal. My primary aim with these stories is not to be flawlessly accurate with historical facts but to help you see from a different perspective. As you read these, try to imagine what the characters must have been thinking and feeling.

STUDY

This section is designed to help you see the connection between the Christmas story and your story. You may be challenged, or you may find a real connection with some of the Christmas characters. My hope is that you'll be able to study your own heart and examine how this piece of the Christmas story intersects with today's world. In this section you will also find intentional questions to prompt personal reflection and group discussion.

SONG

Each chapter contains a Christmas hymn connected to the perspective of that week's character. The way we respond to God when he reveals truth to us is important. It's for that reason that I encourage you to sing these songs with others as you close out your time. May it be like an immediate response of worship that you take before the Lord.

OPTIONAL ACTIVITIES

In the back of the book you will find an optional connect activity for each chapter. These activities are designed with families in mind. Some of you may have children that you would love to bring into this time. These activities are simply tools for you to use as a way of making your kids feel connected to the Christmas story. They might spark great conversation or even create a fun memory. Feel free to use them, tweak them, or just ignore them!

1

SCRIPTURE

After Jesus was born in Bethlehem of Judea in the days of King Herod, wise men from the east arrived in Jerusalem, saying, "Where is he who has been born king of the Jews? For we saw his star at its rising and have come to worship him."

When King Herod heard this, he was deeply disturbed, and all Jerusalem with him. So he assembled all the chief priests and scribes of the people and asked them where the Christ would be born.

"In Bethlehem of Judea," they told him, "because this is what was written by the prophet:

And you, Bethlehem, in the land of Judah, are by no means least among the rulers of

Judah: Because out of you will come a ruler who will shepherd my people Israel."

Then Herod secretly summoned the wise men and asked them the exact time the star appeared. He sent them to Bethlehem and said, "Go and search carefully for the child. When you find him, report back to me so that I too can go and worship him."

After hearing the king, they went on their way. And there it was—the star they had seen at its rising. It led them until it came and stopped above the place where the child was. When they saw the star, they were overwhelmed with joy. Entering the house, they saw the child with Mary his mother, and falling to their knees, they worshiped him. Then they opened their treasures and presented him with gifts: gold, frankincense, and myrrh. And being warned in a dream not to go back to Herod, they returned to their own country by another route.

Then Herod, when he realized that he had been outwitted by the wise men, flew into a rage. He gave orders to massacre all the boys in and around Bethlehem who were two years old and under, in keeping with the time he had learned from the wise men. Then what was spoken through Jeremiah the prophet was fulfilled:

A voice was heard in Ramah, weeping, and great mourning, Rachel weeping for her children; and she refused to be consoled, because they are no more.

-Matthew 2:1-12, 16-18

STORY

As the curtains of our story pull back, we see a king sitting on his throne — a throne that he's commanded for years. He's comfortable there; he feels safe and powerful there. He's spent a lifetime clawing his way to the top and gaining the favor of those who matter most. Year after year he's watched his kingdom expand, his fortunes rise, and his name grow loftier. As we peer in on him sitting on his throne, it's as if we can see him gloriously replaying every past victory. His lips spread into a soft grin as he remembers all those who feebly attempted to stand in his way. He's proud of where he is and he'd do anything necessary to stay there. This king was one of the greatest builders in antiquity. He was no stranger to opposition and no amateur at establishing a kingdom, swaying public opinion, or forcefully securing power and respect. He's done a lifetime's worth of brown-nosing, bribery, murder, and manipulation. He has executed numerous family members including his own wife and three sons. His contemporaries would jest that it was safer to be a pig in this king's family than to be a son.[2] He was hands down the most powerful man of his time and yet beyond the facade stood an utterly paranoid man, petrified of losing an inch of his kingdom.

But on this day, a new challenger came upon the king's radar — an outsider, one that he hadn't seen coming, and one that had drawn the attention of worshippers from foreign lands. As these foreigners from the east came looking for the soon-to-be heir apparent, once again the demon of pride and fear awoke within the king's heart. The paranoia returned. He was the king, he had the power, there could be no other. He knew he had to squelch this narrative of a newborn king immediately. He had seen this before; he knew how to handle these situations. Any threat to his throne and his kingdom would receive no mercy — son, wife, newborn child — it didn't matter. All would fear and remember the name of King Herod — at all costs.

The king's rage met with his instinct as he shouted an all too familiar set of instructions to his soldiers, *"Grab your swords! Slaughter every baby boy in Bethlehem!"*

---

[2] Macrobius, *Saturnalia*, 2:4:11.

STUDY

King Herod was a ruthless king — a man with no restraint, a paranoid and power hungry maniac. His story reads more like a comic book supervillain — it seems too brutal to be true. In the midst of his mania, he was simultaneously masterful. He could build fortresses and temples like no one had seen, and he knew just the right buttons to push to gain the favor of emperors and subjects alike. He wasn't hiding his wickedness from anyone, but like a crafty politician, he provided just the right incentives to keep everybody happy. All in all, Herod was a pro's pro at one thing: kingdom building.

Jesus, the proclaimed newborn King of the Jews, posed one thing to Herod: a threat. He knew the simple biological truth that boys grow up to be men. And if this baby was already drawing worship and adoration as a king, how much more would he draw that attention as he grew up? Like his sons, Herod knew Jesus was another threat to his fame, reputation, and throne.

And Herod was absolutely right.

As savage as he was, Herod's self-exalting spirit is inside all of us too. We too build our name, our fortune, our kingdom. We may not go to the full extent Herod did, but we make compromises and dismiss anything attempting to loosen our iron tight grip on our kingdom. We'll lie to protect our image, we'll be quick to seize control of the narrative, and we'll tear down those who don't support our kingdom.

Jesus wasn't just a threat to Herod; Jesus is a threat to every one of us. He's a threat to our pride, our success, our glory, our fame, our plans. He tells us this when he says, "No one can serve two masters, since either he will hate one and love the other, or he will be devoted to one and despise the other" (Matthew 6:24). We will follow Jesus or we will follow something else, not both. It's him or nothing. So, Herod is actually right, Jesus is a threat. But he's a threat to something that needs to die within all of us — the unquenchable appetite to glorify *our* name. The untamable beast in our souls that must have control of the plan. The unrelenting freight train of pride in our hearts that demolishes all that stands in the way of our hopes and dreams.

But the beauty of the gospel is that as we lay aside our kingdom and our name, and come to him empty-handed to enter into his kingdom, he fills our hands with every imaginable blessing in Christ. Every ounce of acceptance, value, love, joy, happiness, fulfillment, and meaning that we long for can be found in him. Many will hear the truth of Jesus and rightly recognize the threat he poses to their kingdoms. And many will seek to "kill and destroy" him by suppressing the truth with their unrighteousness (Romans 1:18). But today, may you not only see the threat Jesus poses to your sinful desires, but the offer he makes of something so much better. He is the true king who invites you into a new kingdom. One where you don't have to be the hero, because you already have the greatest hero. One where you don't have to secure your own value or position, because you are immeasurably valued by Christ. A kingdom where you don't have to carry the burden of having everything under control, because in Christ, you have the most loving and perfect king leading you.

As you prepare for this Christmas season, may you see the invitation from Jesus to step into his kingdom and engage in building a heavenly kingdom that has no end.

1. What lengths have you gone to/will you go to in order to build and protect your name, fame, and fortune?
2. How does the prospect of surrendering to Jesus pose a threat to your kingdom?
3. Take a few minutes to write down the ways you are seeking to build up your name. Then, open your hands before the Lord. Confess those to him and experience the beauty of going to God empty handed.
4. Read Ephesians 1:3-14 and be reminded of how Jesus fills your hands with blessings.

SONG

Come Thou Long Expected Jesus by Charles Wesley

Come, Thou long expected Jesus,
　　Born to set Thy people free;
　　From our fears and sins release us;
　　Let us find our rest in Thee.
　　Israel's strength and consolation,
　　Hope of all the earth Thou art;
　　Dear desire of every nation,
　　Joy of every longing heart.

Born Thy people to deliver,
　　Born a child, and yet a king,
　　Born to reign in us forever,

Now Thy gracious kingdom bring.
By Thine own eternal Spirit,
Rule in all our hearts alone;
By Thine all sufficient merit,
Raise us to Thy glorious throne.

2

Angels

SCRIPTURE

In the same region, shepherds were staying out in the fields and keeping watch at night over their flock. Then an angel of the Lord stood before them, and the glory of the Lord shone around them, and they were terrified. But the angel said to them, "Don't be afraid, for look, I proclaim to you good news of great joy that will be for all the people: Today in the city of David a Savior was born for you, who is the Messiah, the Lord. This will be the sign for you: You will find a baby wrapped tightly in cloth and lying in a manger."

Suddenly there was a multitude of the heavenly host with the angel, praising God and saying:

> *Glory to God in the highest heaven,*
> *and peace on earth to people he favors!*

–Luke 2:8–14

STORY

The day was finally here! The day of all days! It was time to share the news – the best news! God was unfolding the next chapter of his rescue story, and he called on one of his trusted angels to announce the chapter title.

Angels are no strangers to passing along God's messages. That's their nature; that's what they do. As this angel got the call, the honor was not lost on him. He knew the importance of a task like this. Without hesitation, he followed instructions and made his way down to creation.

As he exited the gates of heaven, his mind started racing. "How will God accomplish this marvelous miracle? King Jesus is going to be a baby?!" The thought baffled him. He had never seen Jesus in such a lowly, humble position. He'd only ever seen him in all his glory, all of the time. Every moment of every day, he and the rest of the angels would marvel at Jesus' radiance, his splendor, his majesty, and his power. He's their Lord, their Master, their King. He's the one that they watch hold all things together in his hands. He's the one they see perform miracle after miracle in the lives of unsuspecting humans. He's the one that they fix their eyes on as he hears, sees, knows, and cares for the heart of everyone in existence. That's their Jesus — the one whom they worship and follow at all times with no question.

But on this day, *that* Jesus becomes a *baby*. And *this* angel gets to share the good news of that rescue coming to Earth. Kinetic anticipation flows through him as he prepares to burst open the night sky and shock the sleepy shepherds. Intrigue bubbles in his gut as to what God could possibly be up to by sending such a grand declaration to the quiet, vacant hillsides of Bethlehem.

Just before he pierces through the cloud cover, he looks back over his shoulder, vision tilted slightly upward towards the heavens. He surveys the thousands upon thousands of fellow warriors eager to burst in behind him to join in the announcement. In all of his excitement, he had forgotten about the army's chorus that was to follow his declaration. He looks into the eyes of face after face of his angelic comrades beaming with joy, each one still radiating blinding light from standing in the presence of God's glory. There's an audible buzzing, the sound of thousands of heavenly warriors ready to be shot out of a cannon. His excitement doubles as he feels the announcement bursting its way towards his lips. He turns toward earth, takes one last breath to prepare to shout, and in a single motion explodes through the clouds to awaken the world to the glory of God.

STUDY

We're fascinated by the spiritual realm — the world of angels and demons. You see that fascination with the spiritual bubble up around Halloween when movies and theme parks spend millions on recreating this world for our entertainment. You see it too in the age-old myths passed on of guardian angels watching out for their divinely assigned humans. Our imaginations are captured by the notion that there's an entire spiritual realm all around us and yet completely invisible to us.

Yet for all of our intrigue, it's even more remarkable that the Bible tells us that angels too have their eyes fixed on an almost unbelievable reality — the reality of God's love for sinful humanity.

In speaking about the gospel, Peter says, "These things have now been announced to you through those who preached the gospel to you by the Holy Spirit sent from heaven—angels long to catch a glimpse of these things" (1 Peter 1:12). Did you catch that? Angels long to look, to catch a glimpse of this gospel story of God saving humanity through Jesus' death and resurrection! The angels, who have seen everything there is to see! They've seen miracles, healings, every inch of the spiritual realm, and they've even seen God in his full glory and lived to tell the tale. Even after seeing all of that, the Bible tells us that they marvel at the prospect of just catching a glimpse of the gospel. They can't take their eyes off the way that the Almighty Jesus decided to take the form of a servant and die in the place of sinful man. They can't restrain their amazement at seeing God pour out his wrath on Jesus at the cross, so that he can then pour out abundant grace on us. They could stare all day, wanting to learn more about how good and faithful God's love and forgiveness is for his people. The angels see it so clearly. We have the most unbelievable, most unimaginable, the most irreplaceable gift of all time — an intimate relationship with the Almighty God of the universe.

Angels aren't partakers of the redemption story and yet their attention is captured by it for all eternity. How much more should we, the ones whom God sacrificed everything to redeem, marvel at this gospel love of Jesus? For many of us this gospel story is good, but it's lost its allure. Like a movie we've seen a hundred times, we know all the lines, but we're no longer clamoring to buy a ticket for the midnight showing. We read the stories, sing the songs, hear about the benefits of our relationship with Christ but our hearts are largely unmoved.

This Christmas, may you see the invitation that's extended to you, and have your heart stirred with affection for Christ, maybe even re-stirred. Let the angels' awe lead you in worship and open your eyes to Christ's glory. Let their announcement be like a megaphone to your soul and their chorus be like a fresh pair of glasses to rightly see the beauty of the gospel.

But as this happens, may our worship surpass that of the angels — for we are the sons and daughters of God! We are the recipients of his grace. We are the ones who have had our sins wiped clean. We are the orphan children who have been adopted by a perfect Father. He was born that *we* may no longer die. So this Christmas, may *we*, the beneficiaries of God's saving grace, take our place as the lead heralds, and proclaim the glory of God to a sleepy world!

1. When was the last time you felt an excitement about the gospel?
2. What aspects of God's love for you have you grown a bit calloused towards?
3. The angels exist to give glory to God. The truth is, that's why we exist too. What tends to drive you to seek glory for yourself rather than give glory to God?
4. Spend a few minutes in prayer just giving God glory, praise, and worship for who he is and what he has done. During this time, try to keep yourself from making requests or praying for others. Just simply remember who he is and give him glory.

SONG

Hark! The Herald Angels Sing! by Charles Wesley

Hark! The herald angels sing,
  Glory to the newborn King;
  Peace on earth, and mercy mild,
  God and sinners reconciled!
  Joyful, all ye nations, rise,
  Join the triumph of the skies;
  With th'angelic host proclaim,
  Christ is born in Bethlehem!

Refrain:
  Hark! The herald angels sing,
  Glory to the newborn King!

Christ, by highest heaven adored,
  Christ the everlasting Lord!
  Come, Desire of Nations, come,
  Fix in us thy humble home.
  Veiled in flesh the God-head see;
  Hail th'Incarnate Deity,
  Pleased as man with men to dwell,
  Jesus, our Emmanuel! [Refrain]

Hail, the heav'n-born Prince of Peace!
  Hail, the Sun of Righteousness!
  Light and life to all he brings,
  Risen with healing in his wings;
  Mild he lays his glory by,

13

Born that man no more may die,
Born to raise the sons of earth,
Born to give them second birth; [Refrain]

3

Shepherds

SCRIPTURE

When the angels had left them and returned to heaven, the shepherds said to one another, "Let's go straight to Bethlehem and see what has happened, which the Lord has made known to us."

They hurried off and found both Mary and Joseph, and the baby who was lying in the manger. After seeing them, they reported the message they were told about this child, and all who heard it were amazed at what the shepherds said to them. But Mary was treasuring up all these things in her heart and meditating on them. The shepherds returned, glorifying and praising God for all the things they had seen and heard, which were just as they had been told.

–Luke 2:15–20

STORY

They still couldn't see a thing. Vigorously they rubbed their eyes and opened them again trying to find their bearings. The light from the angels was so bright that their eyes were still burning and desperately attempting to readjust to the darkness of the countryside. They weren't used to any light out here, they weren't used to much of anything other than the sheep, the darkness, the quiet, and the occasional predator looking for a quick meal.

As the blurry silhouettes of the flock started to come into focus and their vision normalized, an unfamiliar rush came over the shepherds — one that they hadn't really ever known before. They felt *chosen.*

These shepherds never grew up dreaming they would become the protectors of these helpless animals. If they were honest, it wasn't something they wanted to spend their life doing. It gave them a livelihood, but the baggage that came with it was tough to get used to. It was lonely, dirty, dangerous, and degrading. Because of the very nature of their job, the religious folk perpetually labeled them as unclean. They knew the sheep loved them, but they weren't sure about many others outside of that. Spending most of their days in the wilderness, they had no real voice or presence in the world. It was easy at times to wonder if anyone even remembered they were out there. But now, perhaps for the first time, they felt seen, and known, and loved. But most of all *chosen.*

God had chosen to speak to them, the forgotten, the ignored, the voiceless. He had chosen these lowly shepherds to receive the news of great joy! And in an instant everything felt different. It was as if nothing else mattered except what had just happened. By now many of the sheep were starting to wander off, which would have normally prompted an immediate response from these men, but not this time. On this night, God had thrust these shepherds onto center stage. They were now primetime characters in the story God wrote before the world began. That weight was not lost on them as they locked eyes with each other. They knew that this was now their primary, most important job. They had to go see this baby boy! This new job description didn't feel like a duty, it was the most joyful privilege they had ever carried. A job they wanted with their whole hearts! And so they ran. With joy-filled hearts and nervous anticipation they ran to see this child. All the while cherishing that they would be numbered among the first ones to meet and celebrate the newborn King of Kings. Good news of great joy indeed was here.

STUDY

"God has chosen what is foolish in the world to shame the wise, and God has chosen what is weak in the world to shame the strong." -1 Corinthians 1:27

The foolish and the weak. That's who God often hand picks for himself. And it's evidenced so clearly in the shepherds' story. Because when God chooses, it's never based on merit. It's always based on his grace. He chooses those whom he wants to choose.

The Apostle Paul reminds us of this when he says, "For he tells Moses, I will show mercy to whom I will show mercy, and I will have compassion on whom I will have compassion. So then, it does not depend on human will or effort but on God who shows mercy" (Romans 9:15-16). So when God chose the shepherds, it's crystal clear in Scripture that the glory belongs to God. It is simply because of his mercy that he chose them for this honor. And God's choosing is never followed up by silence or complacency, rather it is always accompanied by faith and action.

In Luke 2, the shepherds' simple faith in the words that God entrusted to them, birthed two profound responses. First, they ran to Jesus, and then, they ran to share with all who would listen. Their faith propelled them to move. They were so honored to be chosen by God that they *had* to leave their sheep and see this newborn Savior. Their faith moved not only their hearts but their feet to run and meet Christ. God made his move and poured out his abundant grace and elected them to be his mouthpieces. Then, as his chosen ones, they ran with reckless abandon, leaving behind their duties, to worship their Lord and Savior. In this we see a beautiful reminder: as we receive the undeserved grace of God poured out on us, it fuels us to worship him. It drives us to sacrifice what seems wise to the world in order to be close to Jesus. It gives us the courage to intentionally choose loss in order to gain something more valuable. The gospel opens our eyes to see and opens our hearts to believe that there is nothing better than being with Jesus.

But the story doesn't stop there for the shepherds; their faith also moved them to further action. They had to see the baby. But now that they had seen him, there was a joyful eagerness that wouldn't leave them. They couldn't just go back to the sheep, they could feel it in their bones. They couldn't keep this news to themselves. The news was *so* good, so overwhelmingly good that they would feel crippled if they didn't shout this message from the mountains. And so they did. God had chosen them not just to be recipients of joy but also heralds of it!

What an honor! These voiceless shepherds would be the voices of pronouncement for the greatest news. Dirty, humble countrymen would fill the streets with great joy. Those without influence would be the ones to make an unforgettable impact on any who would listen. In this short episode with the shepherds we see the paradox of the gospel on display. God announces his message of power through the weak and lowly shepherds. And he sends the Almighty Alpha and Omega as a small, vulnerable, and fragile baby boy to bring powerful rescue.

"As it is written: How beautiful are the feet of those who bring good news" (Romans 10:15).

Let's be honest, shepherds aren't beautiful. And their feet *definitely* aren't winning any awards for their appearance. But they've been made beautiful because of who they belong to. They have become beautiful because their feet now carry good news of great joy. The dirt that cakes their feet is now lovely because it represents towns, communities, and people who have now heard the news of Jesus.

The shepherds' journey, in a very similar way, represents many of our journeys. And their calling represents many of our callings as well. If you're in Christ, you can be confident today that God has chosen you. He has chosen you to be part of his story. He has bestowed upon you the honor of being in relationship with him. This was not based on your effort or merit, but because of his mercy. And as his chosen, may you continue to respond in faith this day. Like the shepherds, may you run to worship Jesus. May you look down to be reminded that your feet are beautiful and then run to proclaim the good news of great joy to your community. And as you do, know that you are taking your place in the continuation of the Christmas story.

1. When was a time that you felt chosen by someone? What was

that like?

2. Have you ever had to walk away from something, like the shepherds did the sheep, because it hindered your worship of Jesus? What was that like?

3. How do you think it felt for the shepherds to share the news with their community? What kind of fears or insecurities might they have been wrestling with?

4. What fears or insecurities do you struggle with in being a herald of this message? How can God's choosing of you be a comfort in those struggles?

5. Who is someone in your life that needs to hear you share this good news of great joy?

SONG

Silent Night by Jospeh Mohr

Silent night, holy night,
　All is clam, all is bright
　'Round yon virgin mother and child.
　Holy infant so tender and mild,
　Sleep in heavenly peace,
　Sleep in heavenly peace.

Silent night, holy night,
　Shepherds quake at the sight.
　Glories stream from heaven afar,
　heav'nly hosts sing, "Alleluia!
　Christ the Savior is born!
　Christ the Savior is born!"

Silent night, holy night,
    Son of God, love's pure light
    radiant beams from Thy holy face
    with the dawn of redeeming grace,
    Jesus, Lord, at Thy birth!
    Jesus, Lord, at Thy birth!

Silent night, holy night,
    Wondrous star, lend thy light;
    with the angels let us sing
    "Alleluia" to our King:
    "Christ the Savior is born!
    Christ the Savior is born."

4

Mary

SCRIPTURE

In the sixth month, the angel Gabriel was sent by God to a town in Galilee called Nazareth, to a virgin engaged to a man named Joseph, of the house of David. The virgin's name was Mary. And the angel came to her and said, "Greetings, favored woman! The Lord is with you." But she was deeply troubled by this statement, wondering what kind of greeting this could be. Then the angel told her: "Do not be afraid, Mary, for you have found favor with God. Now listen: You will conceive and give birth to a son, and you will name him Jesus. He will be great and will be called the Son of the Most High, and the Lord God will give him the throne of his father David. He will reign over the house of Jacob forever, and his kingdom will have no end."

Mary asked the angel, "How can this be, since I have not had sexual relations with a man?"

The angel replied to her: "The Holy Spirit will come upon you, and the power of the Most High will overshadow you. Therefore, the holy one to be born will be called the Son of God. And consider your relative Elizabeth—even she has conceived a son in her old age, and this is the sixth month for her who was called childless. For nothing will be impossible with God."

"I am the Lord's servant," said Mary. "May it be done to me according to your word." Then the angel left her.

-Luke 1:26-38

STORY

With every step a shock of tension pulsated throughout her whole body. At this point the exhaustion wasn't a concern anymore. She was stiff, not wanting to move too much out of fear it might send her body into full-blown active labor. She held tightly to the donkey's cloth saddle as she watched her soon-to-be husband saunter away from another house. Joseph had been sure that they would have found a place to stay by now. After all, this was his hometown. But it seemed as if no one wanted him and Mary around. Maybe these families truly had no room, or maybe they just didn't want to associate with the betrothed teenagers who were allegedly pregnant "by the Holy Spirit."

Heaviness fell over Mary as they walked to the last home on the edge of town. She couldn't bear the burden of another rejection. She leaned her body weight on the neck of the donkey, both legs draped to the animal's left side. It was an emotional heaviness — one that came with the responsibility of raising the Messiah. How could they raise the most important child ever born if they couldn't even find a place to sleep? How could they be faithful to nurture and protect the Savior of the world if they couldn't even provide shelter? This was the long awaited Deliverer, surely he deserves better than this. Mary wrestled back and forth with these doubts. She was so distraught and discouraged. Why was this so difficult? But in the midst of her anxious thoughts, she knew that they weren't alone — God was still there. Her fears never lasted long, for she was confident in God's plan. The importance of her calling to be the Messiah's mother never left her. It was an honor, but it was a heavy honor and she knew she needed the Lord's hand.

By now Joseph was approaching the door of the final house. The home was small, not much to it from the looks of the outside. The path to the porch was worn and all was dark except for a flickering orange glow radiating from just underneath the door. It was clear from the surrounding aroma that livestock were somewhere around back. As she heard Joseph's gentle knock she turned her eyes toward the heavens and whispered three simple words: "Lord, help us." She had never felt so desperate for the Lord's intervention. It felt like just a moment but by the time she glanced back toward the door, all she could see was Joseph's face beaming with joy as he tied the donkey up and ushered Mary around back. In an instant, a rush of warmth and comfort washed over Mary. The Lord had provided. She was assured that this responsibility is not hers to carry alone. And as she felt the Lord's presence she placed her hands on her tummy and treasured this moment in her heart.

STUDY

Mary experienced a foreign reality that no other human being ever will — the King of the universe was dependent on her.

24

And yet simultaneously, as Colossians 1 says, all things in the universe were being held together by Christ. The intricacies of the incarnation can make our brains hurt sometimes. But we do know Mary was chosen to nurture and care for the Almighty God in baby form, and because of that, no one adored Jesus quite like Mary. He was her King and yet, as her little boy, he needed her protection. He was her Savior and yet, as her son, he needed her to stabilize his infant head. Mary cherished her little boy as she was probably filled with anticipation of what he would become. Her mind possibly filled with all the things his future would hold — all the beauty and glory and honor waiting for him in the years to come. It wouldn't be long before she realized that there would also be tremendous danger and suffering awaiting him. Yet the Bible tells us in Luke 2:19 that as Mary saw her baby boy, she treasured these things up in her heart. Oh, the abundance of moments that Mary was able to store up and cling to. If we could see with her eyes, surely we would be filled with amazement at how rich these moments were between Mary and Jesus. And Mary knew how special this was, she treasured this calling.

But Mary isn't the only one who's been given something to treasure. We too, as followers of Jesus, are to treasure the gospel. We've been given the gift of Jesus as our Savior and our King as well! And it's a gift so rich and so abundant that it's our treasure! It's a gift so sweet that it changes not only the course of our lives but our eternities. And it's a treasure that must be guarded just like Mary guarded the baby Jesus.

As we read the New Testament we see that Paul instructs Timothy, "Follow the pattern of the sound words that you have heard from me, in the faith and love that are in Christ Jesus. By the Holy Spirit who dwells within us, guard the good deposit entrusted to you" (2 Timothy 1:13-14). In this letter Paul *urges* Timothy, and us too, to guard the gospel, and to do so fervently as if the very message has been entrusted into our care. Mary was the one woman that God chose to entrust his Son to. There was nothing about Mary that made her lovely or worthy to be chosen, but God in his grace, chose to lay this calling on her. And in the same way, God has entrusted Jesus to his people through the good news of the gospel. And as his people, we must feel the weight of that, desire to steward it well, and guard that good deposit.

What does it mean for us to guard the gospel? It means we must preach its message to our hearts everyday, consistently having our faith renewed again and again. It means that we must combat the lies of the enemy with the truths of the gospel. It means that we must say no to anything and everything that competes with it. There will be many who try to convince you to loosen your grip on that deposit or toss it away for something more compelling. Guarding the gospel will cost you. But what you gain by guarding it is of far greater value. Paul says in 2 Corinthians 8:9, "For you know the grace of our Lord Jesus Christ, that though he was rich, yet for your sake he became poor, so that you by his poverty might become rich." This deposit has made us abundantly rich! It has secured for us everything that our souls long for. Through this gospel an incredible truth is actualized: everything we need, we now have in Christ.

And the comforting truth is, the gospel doesn't *need* your protection in order to remain valid. The gospel is the power of God and nothing can stand against it. No, it doesn't need our protection, rather it's the opposite. We need protection and the gospel provides that for us. Mary wasn't strong enough to be the protector and defender of Jesus, but rather he was ultimately strong enough to be her rescue and protection. The Lord was with Mary every step of the journey providing for every need of hers. And the Lord is the same God for Mary as he is for us today. He is our protector and provider who walks with us every step of the way, providing for our deepest needs. He's entrusted to us the greatest treasure and in doing so, has promised that his presence comes with it. So may we see with the eyes of Mary, one who came long before us, and treasure up these things in our hearts also.

1. How do you imagine it would feel to be entrusted with the Messiah as your child?
2. What has God done for you that maybe you've forgotten to treasure up in your heart? (answered prayer, provision, protection, etc.)
3. If you were honest, what things do you tend to treasure more than the gospel? What often seems better or sweeter than the gospel? (money, success, comfort, etc.)
4. In what ways do you need to "guard the good deposit" that God has entrusted to you?

SONG

O Come, All Ye Faithful by John Francis Wade

O come, all ye faithful, joyful and triumphant
  O come ye, O come ye to Bethlehem;
  Come and behold him born the King of angels;

27

Refrain:
   O come, let us adore him,
   O come, let us adore him,
   O come let us adore him, Christ, the Lord.

Sing, choirs of angels, sing in exultation,
   O sing, all ye bright hosts of heaven above;
   Glory to God, all glory in the highest; [Refrain]

Yea, Lord, we greet thee, born this happy morning,
   Jesus, to thee be all glory given;
   Word of the Father, now in flesh appearing; [Refrain]

5

SCRIPTURE

Then Jesus came from Galilee to John at the Jordan, to be baptized by him. But John tried to stop him, saying, "I need to be baptized by you, and yet you come to me?"

Jesus answered him, "Allow it for now, because this is the way for us to fulfill all righteousness." Then John allowed him to be baptized.

When Jesus was baptized, he went up immediately from the water. The heavens suddenly opened for him, and he saw the Spirit of God descending like a dove and coming down on him. And a voice from heaven said: "This is my beloved Son, with whom I am well-pleased."

–Matthew 3:13–17

STORY

The chaos of the night had all seemed to pass by now. The animals that once stirred with agitation were now resting quietly, their heavy breaths like rhythmic background noise. Exhaustion finally got the best of Mary as she drifted off into a deep rest, the kind she hadn't known for the last nine months. Joseph made his way back to his spot on the ground. He had taken his turn holding Jesus, learning how to best comfort his newborn's midnight fusses, to be gentle with his carpenter hands as he placed the sleeping child back down for a few more hours of sleep. For the first time in a while, it was quiet. Still.

In the midst of the stillness, our eyes are drawn back to the sleeping babe. We notice the manger is no longer visible. All we can see now are two large hands gently holding the newborn King. These hands are like nothing we've ever seen and yet we know these hands. Was there ever a manger at all? Had these hands always been holding baby Jesus? He's safe, comforted, and protected in those hands. Suddenly we realize, these are the hands of his Father — his true Father. These are the hands of God.

As these hands hold this sleeping child we gaze upward to see a proud Father looking down from heaven at his son. Abundant joy beams from his face as he smiles down on this perfect moment. He looks at the face of Jesus and in an instant sees eternity past, present, and future. They're existing in perfect harmony. Father, Son, and Spirit, planning this moment before the world began, bursting with excitement as they speak creation into existence. The cries of a baby turn to cries of a man in agony on the cross. He crushes his beloved Son to make atonement for the sins of the world. A choir of angels shout praises and sing as Jesus rises in victory, the Father's heart soaring with love. Ascension as the Son is welcomed home, the saints roaring the praises of their Redeemer. The small child turns to a warrior King riding on a horse as he returns calling his beloved by name. Hell finished, death defeated, sin disarmed. Church redeemed, grace abounding, truth reigning. Love, joy, sorrow, grace, mercy, mingled and messy in this moment. All falls quiet again. Hush. Awe. Peace. Still.

The Father watches baby Jesus' chest rise and fall, and with every breath, he's filled with the purest form of pride. He's known this moment was coming since eternity past and yet, he's so pleased with his son whom he loves with a love that is incorruptible.

This is God's son. This is Jesus, the newborn King. The Father watches over, protects, and provides for him. His hands will never leave him all the days of his life. But before the work of redemption presses on, God the Father soaks in this moment with a heart full of joy and affection for his boy.

STUDY

We rarely consider the perspective of the Father in the Christmas story. But this is his story. The narrative belongs to him. He's the author and sovereign authority over every little detail. As we consider his perspective it's interesting to note that God the Father speaks only three times throughout the gospels — and he repeats himself twice. And when God repeats himself, it is always significant. At the outset of Jesus' ministry in Luke 3:22 God said, "You are my beloved Son; with you I am well-pleased." And later in his life, at the transfiguration in Luke 9:35, the Father said,

"This is my Son, my Chosen One; listen to him!" This is how he sees Jesus, always. It's almost as if this is the banner hanging over the life of Jesus at all times. Everywhere he goes, he carries with him the full affection of God the Father and a secure identity as his beloved son. That status has been uninterrupted for all of eternity. What a privilege!

Never once in his life has Jesus had to wonder about what God thinks of him. Never once has he had to wrestle with the doubt of whether he was loved or accepted by God the Father. And because he had that identity fully secured, he never had to seek it from anyone else. That means he never spent a moment of his life searching for meaning, value, acceptance in the eyes of other people. Every day on earth he enjoyed perfect relationship with God, perfect relationship with people, and a secure position as God's perfect and beloved Son. What a tremendous freedom!

And yet, here's the shocking reality of Christmas. Jesus was willing to sacrifice all of that privilege and give it to you. At times the Christmas story can feel sweet and innocent. But the Christmas story is ultimately about the crucifixion story. Jesus was born to die. Jesus didn't come to earth to give us a holiday season with peppermint coffee drinks, fun family traditions, and colorfully wrapped boxes to open. He came to earth to receive the due penalty of sin on behalf of his chosen people. He was born to die, so that we could truly live. And on the cross Jesus stripped himself of the perfect status he had always enjoyed. He became the object of God's wrath and he himself became sin. He stepped down from the position of son to the position of enemy, from the position of beloved to the position of hated. He stepped down from the status of righteous to the status of rebellious sinner worthy of death. The quiet Christmas morning is truly all about the chaotic crucifixion afternoon that would secure the forgiveness of all God's children. And in the moment of the incarnation, God the Father sees it all.

In Isaiah 53:10 the Bible tells us that it pleased the Father to crush his son on the cross. Why? Not because God is an evil child abuser, but because it pleased God to pay your debt, so that you might be with him. You see, when God looks at his son in the manger he also sees you — the one he sent his son to save. And if you have entered into the family of God by his grace through faith in Jesus, then hear this: the Father looks at you the same way he looks at Christ. He fixes his eyes on you with all the same love and affection, all the same joy and pleasure. As Jesus rose again and ascended back to heaven he secured for you the same status that he enjoys — beloved sonship. The Father is well pleased with you because of Christ. All the benefits and blessings of sonship that Jesus has, you do too. And it's secure, locked in forever, sealed for all of eternity. There is a banner hanging over your life everywhere you go and it reads: "This is my beloved son, with whom I am well pleased." And it's for *that* reason that we say, Merry Christmas and to God be the glory.

1. Whose affection and approval means the most to you? Why?
2. How would your life change if you didn't have to worry about gaining the approval or acceptance of others?
3. How would your life change if you didn't have to worry about gaining the approval or acceptance of God?
4. As you approach Christmas morning and the exchanging of gifts, consider the gift of Jesus and give God glory before opening gifts.

SONG

Joy to the World! by Isaac Watts

Joy to the world! The Lord is come;
   Let earth receive her King;
   Let ev'ry heart prepare Him room
   And Heav'n and nature sing,
   And Heav'n and nature sing,
   And Heav'n, and Heav'n and nature sing.

Joy to the earth! The Savior reigns;
   Let men their songs employ;
   While fields and floods, rocks, hills and plains
   Repeat the sounding joy,
   Repeat the sounding joy,
   Repeat, repeat the sounding joy.

He rules the world with truth and grace,
   And makes the nations prove
   The glories of His righteousness
   And wonders of His love,
   And wonders of His love,
   And wonders, wonders of his love.

Optional Family Activities

For those that are using this Advent book in a family setting, particularly with children, you may find that group activities are helpful to make this time engaging for all ages. Here are a few ideas to help drive the message of each chapter into the kinetic realm. You may find that some of the activities work great for your family, while others sound like a nightmare. Feel free to tweak, upgrade, ignore, or recreate any of these to fit your crew. Bottom line, show your family that talking about Jesus can be fun. So, enjoy this time, get messy, and make a memory.

1) Herod: Jesus the Threat

Activity: Gingerbread House Competition

Give each family member supplies to make their own unique gingerbread house. Put on some Christmas music and enjoy this fun activity as a family. You can even make this a competition if you'd like.

Once everyone has created their house, you can initiate a conversation to make a connection to this week's reading. Here are a few questions to consider asking:

1. When you look at your gingerbread house, what part are you proudest of?
2. How would it make you feel if someone came and destroyed everything you just built?

3. If you knew someone wanted to destroy your gingerbread house, what would you do to protect it?

Now, help your family members relate to King Herod. You may try saying something like this: King Herod was a great builder too. He spent a lifetime building palaces, temples, and fortresses. Everyone thought Herod had the best kingdom! Just like you want to protect the house you built, Herod does too. And when he hears about a newborn king named Jesus, he becomes worried that his house is going to come crashing down. Herod was afraid that Jesus would be a better king than he was, and he was right.

(If you're on a tight budget, or want to make it unique, try using toast instead of gingerbread!)

2) Angels: Jesus the God

Activity: Paper Snowflakes

Give each family a few pieces of white printer paper and a pair of scissors. Have each person make 3 unique snowflakes. You may want to search online to find out the best way to make paper snowflakes. Give each family member a moment to show off their finished snowflakes. Once you've done this, your goal will be to help your family understand how snowflakes give glory to God. You could say something like this: Every snowflake that falls from the sky is different. This shows us how powerful and creative God is! He makes millions of snowflakes fall at one time and yet all of them are different. God is amazing! When the angels came to announce Jesus' birth to the shepherds they were basically saying, "God is amazing! He is coming to save the world! Wow, God is so powerful!"

Here are a couple of questions to continue the conversation:
1. What do you think is amazing about God?
2. What's something God can do that makes you want to say, "God is awesome"?

Be sure to hang your paper snowflakes as decorations once you're done.

(Tip: Have each family member write their answers to the questions on their snowflake.)

3) Shepherds: Jesus the Savior

Activity: Christmas Delivery

As a family, bake Christmas cookies and decorate them with your favorite toppings. Try getting creative with different shapes and flavors. Once your cookies are finished, ask your family which neighbor they think should get the cookies. Once you've decided which neighbor you want to deliver the cookies to, engage in a conversation with your family about how the shepherds shared the greatest news of all time. You could say something like this: The shepherds received the best news of all time. It was so good that it felt like a gift. And they loved this gift so much that they had to share it with others.

Here are a couple of questions to get the conversation started:
1. Have you ever had something you really wanted to share with someone else?
2. What's the best part about sharing?

Be sure to include a short note with your Christmas delivery.

(Tip: If there's a neighbor you've never met before, use this as an opportunity to meet them and start a relationship!)

4) Mary: Jesus the Baby

Activity: Campout Movie Night

As a family build a fort in your living room using chairs, blankets, and pillows. Then, with popcorn popped, watch your favorite Christmas movie together in the fort. The whole idea with this activity is to make a memory that you can treasure together as a family. You may want to talk with your kids about how God gave Mary many sweet moments as the mother of Jesus that she treasured in her heart. Hopefully, this moment becomes one that you treasure together as a family.

(Tip: If you want to take this to the next level, get an air mattress and make it a family sleepover in the living room.)

5) God: Jesus the Son

Activity: Thank You, Jesus

This chapter will most likely be done on Christmas Eve or Christmas morning. Before you open presents, give each family member a chance to think about one thing they want to thank Jesus for. Give each person a piece of paper and some markers or crayons. Everyone should draw a picture of that one thing. It could be an item, a person, an attribute of God, or even an answered prayer. Once everyone has shared their picture, spend a few minutes praying and thanking God for sending Jesus, the greatest gift of all time. Also, thank him for continuing to give little gifts that remind us of his love.

(Tip: You may want to collect the drawings and save them in a box. If this becomes a family tradition, it will be a fun way to remember what God has done in your family for years to come.)

Made in the USA
Columbia, SC
30 August 2020